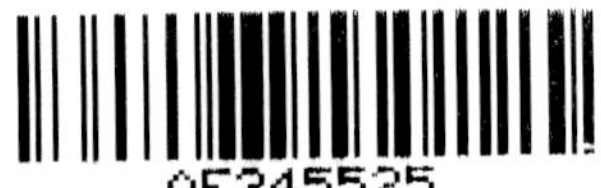

Happy Retirement

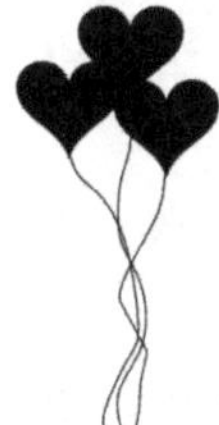

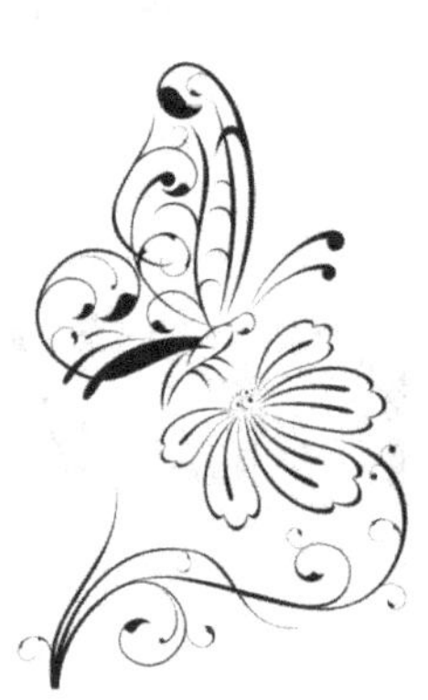

ISBN: 9781912641628

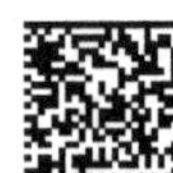

CPSIA information can be obtained
at www.ICGtesting.com
Printed in the USA
BVHW012203030721
611130BV00011B/62

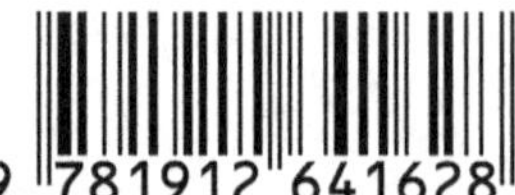